To prohibit cooperation with or assistance to any investigation or prosecution under a universal jurisdiction statute.

United States Congress House of Representatives

108TH CONGRESS
1ST SESSION

H. R. 2050

To prohibit cooperation with or assistance to any investigation or prosecution under a universal jurisdiction statute.

IN THE HOUSE OF REPRESENTATIVES

MAY 9, 2003

Mr. ACKERMAN (for himself and Mr. WEXLER) introduced the following bill; which was referred to the Committee on International Relations

---

A BILL

To prohibit cooperation with or assistance to any investigation or prosecution under a universal jurisdiction statute.

1 *Be it enacted by the Senate and House of Representa-*

2 *tives of the United States of America in Congress assembled,*

3 **SECTION 1. SHORT TITLE.**

4 This Act may be cited as the "Universal Jurisdiction

5 Rejection Act of 2003".

6 **SEC. 2. FINDINGS.**

7 Congress makes the following findings:

8 　　(1) On July 16, 1993, the parliament of Bel-

9 gium adopted a statute, the "Anti-Atrocity Law,"

10 covering grave breaches of the 1949 Geneva Conven-

1 tions and the Additional Protocols I and II of 1977

2 to those Conventions. Under the 1993 law, Belgian

3 courts claim to have jurisdiction over violations of

4 humanitarian law under the Geneva Conventions

5 and Additional Protocols, regardless of the "char-

6 acter" of the conflict, the location of the alleged

7 acts, or the nationality of the victim or alleged per-

8 petrator.

9   (2) In 1999, Belgium's "Anti-Atrocity Law"

10 was amended to include genocide and crimes against

11 humanity to international crimes over which Belgian

12 courts can exercise universal jurisdiction. The 1999

13 amendments adopted the definition of crimes against

14 humanity used in the Rome Statute of the Inter-

15 national Criminal Court, which includes acts such as

16 murder when committed as part of a widespread or

17 systematic attack against civilians.

18   (3) On June 18, 2001, 23 Lebanese-Palestinian

19 nationals brought a petition to Belgium's Attorney

20 General filing a criminal complaint under Belgium's

21 "Anti-Atrocity Law" against Israeli Prime Minister

22 Ariel Sharon, former Director-General of the Israeli

23 Ministry of Defense Amos Yaron, and "all other per-

24 sons whether Lebanese or Israeli whose responsi-

25 bility will be established during the course of the in-

1 vestigation," alleging their complicity with the

2 Phalangist massacres of Palestinians in the Sabra

3 and Shatila refugee camps in Lebanon in 1982.

4 (4) The suit against Prime Minister Sharon—

5 (A) is politically motivated—

6 (i) since the events concerned took

7 place in 1982, the Belgian "Anti-Atrocity

8 Law" was passed in 1993 and amended in

9 1999, and the proceedings were only com-

10 menced in 2001 after Ariel Sharon became

11 Prime Minister of Israel; and

12 (ii) since the issue of the Sabra and

13 Shatila massacres was already examined by

14 the Kahan Commission, established by the

15 Government of Israel on September 28,

16 1982, under section 4 of Israel's Commis-

17 sions of Inquiry Law of 1968;

18 (B) is an assault on the internationally ac-

19 cepted concept of state sovereignty since neither

20 the plaintiffs nor the defendants have any con-

21 nection to Belgium whatsoever, and there is no

22 claim that any crime has been committed on

23 Belgian soil or against Belgian nationals; and

24 (C) is an assault on the internationally rec-

25 ognized legal principle regarding the inadmis-

1 sibility of prosecution under ex post facto legis-
2 lation.

3 (5) On September 5, 2001, the Belgian Inves-
4 tigating Magistrate decided that he had no jurisdic-
5 tion to investigate the suit.

6 (6) On June 26, 2002, the Belgian Court of
7 Appeals ruled the complaint against Prime Minister
8 Sharon, et al., was "not admissible because of the
9 principle of Belgian law that crimes committed in
10 other countries cannot be prosecuted in Belgium un-
11 less the author or presumed author has been found
12 in Belgium".

13 (7) In January 2003, the Belgian Chief Pros-
14 ecutor for the Appellate Court (Chamber of Indict-
15 ments), in the legal opinion he gave to the Supreme
16 Court justices, unambiguously pointed out that the
17 general principle governing universal jurisdiction—
18 "extradite or prosecute"—implies that the defendant
19 must be present in the territory of a prosecuting
20 state and cited the Geneva Conventions, which also
21 require the presence of the defendant. The Belgian
22 Chief Prosecutor for the Appellate Court argued fur-
23 ther that conducting such proceedings in absentia
24 would be prejudicial to the rights of the defense, and
25 even warned against rendering the Belgian legal sys-

1 tem a "virtual" forum for frivolous prosecutions if
2 complainants were not required to prove a link to
3 Belgium. The Belgian Chief Prosecutor for the Ap-
4 pellate Court further recommended to the Supreme
5 Court that it should reject the suit.

6 (8) On February 12, 2003, the Belgian Su-
7 preme Court (Cour de Cassation) reversed the Bel-
8 gian Court of Appeals and decided that Belgium in-
9 deed has jurisdiction to hear the case against Prime
10 Minister Sharon et al., even in the absence of any
11 link to Belgium. With regard to Prime Minister
12 Sharon, the Belgian Supreme Court decided that
13 further proceedings against him should be post-
14 poned, since he presently enjoys immunity due to his
15 position as Prime Minister, but that proceedings
16 may continue against him when he is no longer in
17 office. With regard to former Director-General of the
18 Israeli Ministry of Defense Amos Yaron and any
19 other defendants, the Belgian Supreme Court held
20 that proceedings against them can continue as nor-
21 mal.

22 (9) On March 18, 2003, seven Iraqi families,
23 together with a nongovernmental organization that
24 opposes current United States policy toward Iraq,
25 filed suit in the Belgian courts under Belgium's

1 "Anti-Atrocity Law" against President George H.W.

2 Bush, Vice-President Richard B. Cheney, Secretary

3 of State Colin L. Powell, and General H. Norman

4 Schwarzkopf (U.S. Army-Ret.), alleging their re-

5 sponsibility for war crimes during the 1991 Persian

6 Gulf War.

7 (10) On April 2, 2003, the Chamber of Rep-

8 resentatives of Belgium, by a vote of 63–48, amend-

9 ed and circumscribed Belgium's "Anti-Atrocity

10 Law" to require a nexus between Belgium and the

11 alleged warcrime or atrocity.

12 (11) On April 4, 2003, the Senate of Belgium

13 failed to adopt the amendments adopted by the Bel-

14 gian Chamber of Representatives on April 2, 2003.

15 (12) On April 5, 2003, the Senate of Belgium

16 approved the amendments adopted by the Belgian

17 Chamber of Representatives on April 2, 2003. As

18 amended, the Belgian "Anti-Atrocity Law" allows

19 the Belgian Minister of Justice, in cases in which

20 the alleged victim is not Belgian and the accused's

21 home state upholds the right of a fair trial, to inter-

22 vene and refer the complaint to that state. Further,

23 the amended law provides that before a victim can

24 file a case directly in the future, there must be some

25 link with Belgium, whether because the suspect is on

1 Belgian soil, because the alleged crimes took place in
2 Belgium, or because the victim is Belgian or has
3 lived in Belgium for at least three years.

4   (13) A growing number of countries have
5 adopted universal jurisdiction acts which authorize
6 the national judicial or prosecutorial authorities of a
7 country to investigate, prosecute, and punish geno-
8 cide, war crimes, acts of torture, violations of human
9 rights, or crimes against humanity not involving any
10 of the nationals or property of that country, or that
11 did not occur on the territory of that country or ter-
12 ritory under its control.

13   (14) Implicit within the very concept of uni-
14 versal jurisdiction is a threat to the sovereignty of
15 the United States. There now exists the possibility
16 that foreign courts claiming universal jurisdiction
17 could entertain suits brought by third-country na-
18 tionals against members of the Armed Forces of the
19 United States and the President and other senior
20 elected and appointed officials of the United States
21 Government. No less than members of the Armed
22 Forces of the United States, senior officials of the
23 United States Government deserve the full protec-
24 tion of the United States Constitution with respect

1   to official actions taken by them to protect the na-

2   tional interests of the United States.

SEC. 3. POLICY OF THE UNITED STATES CONCERNING CLAIMS OF UNIVERSAL JURISDICTION.

5   It is the policy of the United States to reject any

6   claim of universal jurisdiction made by foreign govern-

7   ments and to refuse to render any assistance or support

8   to any foreign government pursuing an investigation or

9   prosecution under a universal jurisdiction act.

SEC. 4. PROHIBITION ON COOPERATION WITH ANY INVESTIGATION OR PROSECUTION UNDER A UNIVERSAL JURISDICTION ACT.

13   (a) CONSTRUCTION.—The provisions of this sec-

14   tion—

15   (1) apply only to cooperation with investigations

16   and prosecutions under a universal jurisdiction act

17   and shall not be construed to apply to cooperation

18   with an ad hoc international criminal tribunal estab-

19   lished by the United Nations Security Council before

20   or after the enactment of this Act to investigate and

21   prosecute war crimes committed in a specific country

22   or during a specific conflict; and

23   (2) shall not be construed to prohibit—

24   (A) any action permitted under section 6;

(B) any other action taken by members of the Armed Forces of the United States outside the territory of the United States while engaged in military operations involving the threat or use of force when necessary to protect such personnel from harm or to ensure the success of such operations; or

(C) communication by the United States to a foreign government of its policy with respect to a particular matter concerning a universal jurisdiction act.

(b) PROHIBITION ON SPECIFIC FORMS OF COOPERATION AND ASSISTANCE.—No agency or entity of the United States Government or of any State or local government, including any court, may cooperate with, provide support (including financial support) for, or provide any other kind of assistance to any investigation or prosecution by a foreign government under a universal jurisdiction act, including by—

(1) taking any action relating to—

(A) the arrest, extradition, or transit of suspects, or the provisional arrest of suspects; or

(B) the seizure of property, forfeiture of assets, execution of searches and seizures, service of warrants, or other judicial process;

(2) the taking, preservation, or transfer of any evidence or testimony; or

(3) the analysis, sharing, or transfer of relevant information or intelligence.

(d) RESTRICTION ON ASSISTANCE PURSUANT TO MUTUAL LEGAL ASSISTANCE TREATIES.—The United States shall exercise its rights—

(1) under any treaty or executive agreement providing for mutual legal assistance in criminal matters,

(2) under any multilateral convention with legal assistance provisions,

(3) under any extradition treaty to which the United States is a party, or

(4) in connection with the execution or issuance of any letter rogatory,

to prevent the use of any assistance provided by the United States under such treaty, agreements, conventions, or letter rogatory in any investigation or prosecution under a universal jurisdiction act.

(d) PROHIBITION ON INVESTIGATIVE ACTIVITIES OF AGENTS.—No agent of a foreign principal pursuing any

1 investigation or prosecution under a universal jurisdiction
2 act may conduct, in the United States or any territory
3 subject to the jurisdiction of the United States, any activ-
4 ity with respect to such investigation or prosecution that
5 relates to a preliminary inquiry, investigation, prosecution,
6 or other proceeding.

7 **SEC. 5. PROHIBITION ON DIRECT OR INDIRECT TRANSFER**
8 **OF CERTAIN CLASSIFIED NATIONAL SECU-**
9 **RITY INFORMATION.**

10 (a) DIRECT TRANSFER.—The President shall ensure
11 that appropriate procedures are implemented to prevent
12 the transfer to foreign judicial or prosecutorial authorities
13 of classified national security information that is relevant
14 to any investigation or prosecution under a universal juris-
15 diction act.

16 (b) INDIRECT TRANSFER.—The President shall en-
17 sure that appropriate procedures are implemented to pre-
18 vent the transfer, to the government of any country that
19 is cooperating with an investigation or prosecution under
20 a universal jurisdiction act, of classified national security
21 information that is relevant to matters under such inves-
22 tigation or prosecution by foreign judicial or prosecutorial
23 authorities, unless that government has provided written
24 assurances to the President that such information will not

1 be made available for any use in such investigation or
2 prosecution.

3   (c) CONSTRUCTION.—The provisions of this section
4 shall not be construed to prohibit any action permitted
5 under section 6.

SEC. 6. AUTHORITY TO FREE MEMBERS OF THE ARMED FORCES OF THE UNITED STATES AND CERTAIN OTHER PERSONS HELD CAPTIVE FOR INVESTIGATION OR PROSECUTION UNDER A UNIVERSAL JURISDICTION ACT.

11   (a) AUTHORITY.—The President may use all means
12 necessary and appropriate to bring about the release from
13 captivity of any person described in subsection (b) who
14 is being detained or imprisoned against that person's will
15 by reason of any investigation or prosecution under a uni-
16 versal jurisdiction act with respect to actions undertaken
17 by that person in an official capacity as a covered United
18 States person or covered allied person, as the case may
19 be.

20   (b) PERSONS AUTHORIZED TO BE FREED.—The au-
21 thority of subsection (a) applies with respect to the fol-
22 lowing persons:

23   (1) Any covered United States person.

24   (2) Any covered allied person, if the government
25   of the country by reason of which the individual is

1 a covered allied person requests that the authority

2 under subsection (a) be exercised.

3 (3) Any individual detained or imprisoned for

4 official actions taken while the individual was—

5 (A) a covered United States person; or

6 (B) a covered allied person, if the govern-

7 ment of the country by reason of which the in-

8 dividual is a covered allied person requests that

9 the authority under subsection (a) be exercised.

10 (c) AUTHORIZATION OF LEGAL ASSISTANCE.—When

11 any person described in subsection (b) is arrested, de-

12 tained, prosecuted, or imprisoned by reason of any inves-

13 tigation or prosecution under a universal jurisdiction act,

14 the authority under subsection (a) may be used—

15 (1) for the provision of legal representation and

16 other legal assistance to that person (including, in

17 the case of a person entitled to assistance under sec-

18 tion 1037 of title 10, United States Code, represen-

19 tation and other assistance in the manner provided

20 in that section); and

21 (2) for the provision of exculpatory evidence on

22 behalf of that person.

23 (d) BRIBES AND OTHER INDUCEMENTS NOT AU-

24 THORIZED.—Subsection (a) does not authorize the provi-

1 sion of financial incentives to secure the release from cap-

2 tivity of a person described in subsection (b).

3 **SEC. 7. ALLIANCE COMMAND ARRANGEMENTS.**

4 (a) REPORT ON ALLIANCE COMMAND ARRANGE-

5 MENTS.—Not later than 6 months after the date of the

6 enactment of this Act, the President shall transmit to the

7 appropriate congressional committees a report with re-

8 spect to each military alliance to which the United States

9 is party—

10 (1) describing the degree to which members of

11 the Armed Forces of the United States may, in the

12 context of military operations undertaken by or pur-

13 suant to that alliance, be placed under the command

14 or operational control of foreign military officers

15 subject to a universal jurisdiction act because they

16 are nationals of a country that has adopted a uni-

17 versal jurisdiction act; and

18 (2) describing the degree to which members of

19 the Armed Forces of the United States engaged in

20 military operations undertaken by or pursuant to

21 that alliance may be exposed to greater risks of in-

22 vestigation or prosecution under a universal jurisdic-

23 tion act as a result of being placed under the com-

24 mand or operational control of foreign military offi-

1 cers subject to the jurisdiction of a universal juris-

2 diction act.

3 (b) DESCRIPTION OF MEASURES TO ACHIEVE EN-

4 HANCED PROTECTION FOR MEMBERS OF THE ARMED

5 FORCES OF THE UNITED STATES.—Not later than 1 year

6 after the date of the enactment of this Act, the President

7 shall transmit to the appropriate congressional committees

8 a description of modifications to command and operational

9 control arrangements within military alliances to which

10 the United States is a party that could be made in order

11 to reduce any risks to members of the Armed Forces of

12 the United States identified under subsection (a)(2).

13 (c) SUBMISSION IN CLASSIFIED FORM.—The report

14 under subsection (a), and the description of measures

15 under subsection (b), or appropriate parts thereof, may

16 be submitted in classified form.

17 **SEC. 8. WAIVER AND TERMINATION OF PROHIBITIONS OF**

18 **THIS ACT.**

19 (a) AUTHORITY TO INITIALLY WAIVE SECTIONS 4

20 AND 5.—The President may waive the prohibitions and

21 requirements of sections 4 and 5 with respect to any coun-

22 try if the President, at least 15 days before exercising such

23 waiver authority—

1   (1) notifies the appropriate congressional com-
2 mittees of the intention to exercise such authority;
3 and

4   (2) determines and reports to the appropriate
5 congressional committees that the government of
6 that country and the United States have entered
7 into a binding agreement that—

8   (A) prohibits application of the universal
9 jurisdiction act over—

10   (i) covered United States persons,

11   (ii) covered allied persons, and

12   (iii) individuals for acts done while
13 they were covered United States persons or
14 covered allied persons,

15 with respect to actions undertaken by them in
16 an official capacity, and

17   (B) ensures that no person described in
18 subparagraph (A) will be investigated, arrested,
19 detained, prosecuted, or imprisoned by reason
20 of any suit, investigation, or prosecution under
21 the applicable universal jurisdiction act.

22 (b) REPORTS.—

23   (1) REPORTING REQUIREMENT.—The President
24 shall, with respect to the government of each coun-
25 try with which the United States has entered into a

binding agreement under subsection (a)(2), determine and report to the appropriate congressional committees whether that government—

 (A) remains party to, and has continued to abide by, that agreement; and

 (B) has taken no steps to investigate, arrest, detain, prosecute, or imprison any person described in subsection (a)(2)(A) pursuant to the applicable universal jurisdiction act.

(2) TIMING OF REPORTS.—Reports under paragraph (1) shall be submitted—

 (A) not later than 6 months after the date of the enactment of this Act; and

 (B) not later than the end of each 1-year period thereafter.

(c) TERMINATION OF WAIVER PURSUANT TO SUBSECTION (a).—Any waiver exercised under subsection (a) with respect to a country shall terminate if and when a report submitted under subsection (b) contains a determination by the President that the government of that country—

 (1) is no longer a party to, or has not continued to abide by, the agreement with that government under subsection (a)(2); or

1   (2) has taken steps to investigate, arrest, de-

2 tain, prosecute, or imprison any person described in

3 subsection (a)(2)(A) pursuant to the applicable uni-

4 versal jurisdiction act.

SEC. 9. NONDELEGATION.

6   The authorities vested in the President by section 8

7 may not be delegated by the President pursuant to section

8 301 of title 3, United States Code, or any other provision

9 of law.

SEC. 10. DEFINITIONS.

11   In this Act:

12   (1) UNIVERSAL JURISDICTION ACT.—The term

13 "universal jurisdiction act" means a statute of a for-

14 eign country that authorizes its judicial or prosecu-

15 torial authorities to investigate, prosecute, and pun-

16 ish genocide, war crimes, acts of torture, violations

17 of human rights, or crimes against humanity that—

18   (A) at the time of their actual or alleged

19 occurrence, were not committed by or against

20 the citizens or residents of that country or their

21 property;

22   (B) did not occur on the territory of that

23 country or territory under its control; or

24   (C) are otherwise prosecutable by an ad

25 hoc international criminal tribunal established

by the United Nations Security Council for the purpose of prosecuting such acts.

(2) AGENT OF A FOREIGN PRINCIPAL.—The term "agent of a foreign principal" has the meaning given that term in section 1 of the Foreign Agents Registration Act of 1938, as amended (22 U.S.C. 611).

(3) APPROPRIATE CONGRESSIONAL COMMITTEES.—The term "appropriate congressional committees" means the Committee on International Relations of the House of Representatives and the Committee on Foreign Relations of the Senate.

(4) CLASSIFIED NATIONAL SECURITY INFORMATION.—The term "classified national security information" means information that is classified or classifiable under Executive Order 12958 or a successor Executive order.

(5) COVERED ALLIED PERSON.—The term "covered allied person" means any military personnel, elected or appointed official, or other person employed by or working on behalf of the government of a NATO member country, a major non-NATO ally, or Taiwan, for so long as that government has not adopted a universal jurisdiction act.

1   (6) COVERED UNITED STATES PERSON.—The

2 term "covered United States person" means any

3 member of the Armed Forces of the United States,

4 any elected or appointed official of the United States

5 Government, and any other person employed by or

6 working on behalf of the United States Government.

7   (7) MAJOR NON-NATO ALLY.—The term "major

8 non-NATO ally" means a country that has been so

9 designated in accordance with section 517 of the

10 Foreign Assistance Act of 1961.

○